I0133013

An Ordinary Woman's Walk with God

Reva Coker Horton

Dedication

To my dear friends Glenna Grimsley and Helen McCann who gave me love and companionship during a time when I was floundering with depression and hopelessness.

God blessed me when he brought you into my life and without a doubt you were my guardian angels for the duration of the darkness that was associated with those years.

To my children Joe, Gena, Barbara, and Jason who gave me the privilege of being their mother. Without them many of these stories could never be written. Were it possible I would do motherhood all over again and use the valuable lessons you have taught me in raising you to adulthood.

Your love has sustained me in life. You have made me proud.

Then last but not least to my husband Charlie whose encouragement and sense of humor pushed me to achieve my goals and bucket list I set for myself. Without your support I could never have tried much less reached these goals in my life.

Angels in Our House

Christmas was a month away and my children were anxious to put up the little artificial Christmas tree we dug out each year.

With four children to care for and working a full time job at a local bank I could not muster any Christmas spirit nor did I have the energy to dig out all the decorations much less clean up the mess afterward.

Each time the children asked I would put them off saying, "no not tonight," or "I am just too tired." I felt bad each time I refused them, but after working eight to five, preparing a meal, and other usual tasks in taking care of family I could not stop long enough to put the tree up.

Working late one evening I came home and was met at the door being told to shut my eyes as my children led me into the living room.

Upon opening my eyes I saw the Christmas tree was up and decorated. Even the lights were in place and flashing brightly.

Praising and admiring the Christmas tree I remark, "If we had an angel for the top of the tree it would be perfect."

I thought it odd that upon my remark they looked at each other and left the room. I could hear a conversation taking place in the other room after which they emerged with a package in their hands insisting that I open it. I resisted saying that Christmas was not here and was told that they had voted and I should open the package now.

I open the package and lying upon a bed of white tissue paper is an angel for the top of the Christmas tree. I am overwhelmed at what has just transpired and suggest we put the angel on top of the tree. My children are excited as the angel has lights all around its head like a halo.

At last the angel is up and the lights are turned on. "What a beautiful tree," I exclaim and turn to see the happiness and joy on each of their faces as they beam with pride.

It could have been a decorated tree stump but to me I will never know a Christmas that I won't remember those faces and how they looked when the angel lit up and the little lights began flashing around her head.

They are all grown now and have homes of their own, but their mother will always remember this as being the best Christmas present they ever gave her. It was not just the angel on top of the tree. It was their happy shining faces as the wonder of the tree held them in awe.

The angels that night long ago when Christ was born could not have looked at the stars with more wonder that the wonder on the

faces of my children the night the angel
came to our house.

Leaf Love

I love leaves, and in the fall of the year I am in awe of their beauty as I look at the different colors and shapes they become. No other time of the year do I feel the security and beauty surrounding me as I do when the trees begin their winter hibernation and the leaves begin to turn into riots of color.

God knew this of me.

In a despondent mood one morning I walk out to retrieve the morning paper. As I walk with a cloud over my spirit I notice a huge leaf begin floating toward me. This would not be too unusual as we have huge oak trees in our yard, but this is not an oak leaf. It is a beautiful red maple leaf gliding and dancing as it drops to the ground.

I watch in rapt attention as the leaf softly lands at my feet and I reach to pick it up.

Tears sting my eyes at the significance of what I hold. There are no maple trees in this area. We have only oak.

God saw my distress and was telling me how much he loved me with this scarlet leaf. He knew I would receive his message. A beautiful leaf, reminding me I was not alone.

Emergency Room Angel

Working the three to eleven shift in the emergency room of our local hospital I look up to see a little shriveled stooped Black man standing staring at me.

I smile and ask him if I can help him and he does not reply but still stands with his eyes staring like he cannot believe what he is seeing. I become uneasy.

Finally he says, "Mam I am not trying to come on to you, but you looks like an angel and I cannot help but stare."

I am stunned. I touch his wrinkled arm and say that is the nicest thing anyone has ever said to me. He still stares as I tell him he has made my day.

I often reflect on that night and wonder what that man actually saw as he looked at me. Could it be God gave me the countenance of an angel just for that little man to see and feel that he had been given a glimpse into the realm of God or was he my angel giving me hope to keep on having faith and was I given insight into God's realm through him?

Each time I think of this encounter it brings me reassurance that the presence of God can come to each of us in many different forms and that at any time we can be entertained by angels unaware.

I Want To Be Ready

I had cancelled my first reservation to attend a Walk to Emmaus Christian retreat and with pressure from a couple of my friends I had rescheduled. I was thinking I was really wasting my time. I did not want to be here and my friends would tell me later they thought I would not stay the four days of the retreat.

As everyone gathered for the opening program I watched as they helped an elderly lady to her seat in the chapel, and I thought how tired she must be from walking up the hill to the chapel hobbling on her cane.

As the service began I was amazed to see this little lady rise from her seat and announce that she had something to say.

It had been her dream to be able to attend a walk to Emmaus, but she figured she was too old and had not pursued it. Her church heard of her dream and encouraged her to attend. She was excited to be here.

I am 94 years old she went on to say, and I am standing on the edge of this world looking over into the next, and I know it won't be long before I cross over. I have tried to live a godly life and when I cross over I do not want to look back and see any unfinished business I needed to take care of. I want to know all my wrongs have been righted and anything I should have done completed. I want my slate to be clean here on this earth before I go, and I reckon I have talked long enough. I just want to say I'm here to get a blessing.

I reckon there were not many dry eyes that morning when she sat down. My heart was touched and it was as if I heard God saying, I need you to be ready. I have always heard sermons or read the scriptures about being ready, but never have they had the impact as this 94 year old woman's witness who knew time was getting short for her on this earth and wanted to be ready.

How humble I felt. What an attitude adjustment I had in only a few minutes. I found myself smiling and thinking, I reckon I got the blessing today.

Hebrews 10:24-25

Let us consider one another in order to stir up love and good works, not forsaking the assembling of ourselves together, as is the manner of some, but exhorting one another.

I Remember 9-11

September 11, 2001 found me on the road to attend real estate classes in Arlington, Texas.

During my life I have used driving time as praying time and was engaged in this manner when the most overpowering urge came over me to pray for America. This was odd in the fact that I had never thought of praying for our nation before, but now I poured out my heart for America.

Arriving at school I walk into the cafeteria where everyone congregated before class. I see all my classmates hovered around the television watching the morning news. Many of them have looks of shock on their faces as they intently watch. I ask what is going on and they tell me the trade center in New York has been attacked and the safety of our nation is at risk. We are all in denial and cannot believe this is happening.

As I watch I am overly stunned as I remember what happened on my drive to school and the unmistakable commission from on high to pray for America. From that encounter I understand that through all the death, heartache, and pain of 9-11 God was there.

Going Back To the Old Home Church

Our family had decided that we were not getting the spiritual nourishment from the little church we attended so we began attending a charismatic church in another city.

Relatives were upset that we chose to attend another church and wrote letters that were hurtful stating that our ancestors had attended our previous church for generations and thought we should continue.

Months went by and each time I opened my Bible to study it would fall open to a scripture in Mark 5: 19 which reads, "And he did not let him, but he said to him, go home to your people and report to them what great things the Lord has done for you and how he has had mercy on you." Each time I would read the scripture I would think about the church we had left. At last I said to the Lord, "If you want us to go back to that church you open the door and I will walk through it," "I cannot do this by myself."

Later in the week there was a knock on my door. I open it to a gentleman who was a member of the church we had left. As he walks into our home he says to me, "I do not know why I am here, but I would like to ask you to teach my Sunday school class while I am on vacation. Before I could think or give excuses I answered yes.

I am dumfounded by what has just transpired and it is at this time I remember what I had told the Lord. The Lord held me to my vow.

To him I then honored my promise and made my way back to our home church. I did teach the Sunday school class that next Sunday and went on to teach it for the next four years.

God brought a new vitality to that Sunday school class and we grew from a small group to fill a room. What a learning experience. What a revelation that God does speak to us and if we are in tune and open to his call we will receive the message along with a blessing.

It still amazes me after all these years at this touch of God and how he blessed my life when I simply said, "God I can't do this on my own, I need you to go with me."

Hebrews 11:6

Without faith it is impossible to please Him, for he who comes to God must believe that He is, and that He is a rewarder of those who diligently seek him.

Medical Advice

Working the emergency room registration desk in our local hospital I saw many things come through its doors. There was pain, loss, broken hearts, and dreams that walked in and out of those doors each day.

Being the first contact for most of those patients it was important I have patience, empathy, and kindness in this capacity. Sometimes I was successful, sometimes I was not, but I never let that irritation show as I talked with each one.

One night during my shift a lady walks in with major life melt down. She was crying, no reason to live, problems of all kinds, and alone. As I registered her I began talking to her and reassuring her that she was not alone. I shared similar parts of my life with her and she began telling me about herself and the problems she was going through.

Although we shared less than twenty minutes the communication was the crux of what she needed. Someone to listen and make her feel they cared and more than that she needed to hear that her problems were going to work out and she would be ok. I reminded her that I was living proof she would be just fine and that things might not change overnight, but if she calmed down worked toward her goals realizing some of them might take time she would see results.

When she was called to go back to see the doctor she proclaimed, "I don't need to see the doctor now. This lady has helped me and I am going home." Imagine my shock!

I nearly lost my job as the result of her statement as I was accused of giving medical advice. I never gave medical advice I just opened my heart and let her see she was not alone and shared personal experiences that she might know that she would make it.

From this encounter I learned that we all at some time need reinforcement and that we are worthwhile and worthy of love.

Psalms 30:12

Weeping may endure for the night but joy comes with the morning.

Lord You Have To Wake Me Up

Being the mother of four children, keeping a home, and working an eight to five job never allowed me a lot of quiet time to pray and read the word.

One morning while preparing breakfast for my family I remarked to the Lord, "Lord I guess if I am going to get any time with you then you will need to wake me up at 3:00 in the morning."

My husband worked the night shift at a local plant and the kids and I were in bed fast asleep that night when my bed shakes. I rise up thinking it was one of the kids. There is no one there and I lay my head back on the pillow. All at once it seemed as if someone had pushed my head into the pillow. I quickly get up and as I do my eyes lock on to the clock. Three o'clock. I remember what I had said to the Lord and get on my knees.

This is not the end of the story. Again the following night we are in bed asleep and I awake to the most horrible skunk odor just outside my window. The smell is simply overpowering. I rise on my elbow to look at the clock. You guessed it. Three o'clock. The Lord was seeking my time with him.

I learned a valuable lesson from this experience and it was that the Lord does have a sense of humor and he does want to spend time with his children even if he has to wake you up at three o'clock in the morning.

Maybe God is summoning you to spend some time with him, and if it is in the wee morning hours you certainly will not have any interruptions.

God wants us to desire to spend time with him. God knows our thoughts, but he responds to our prayers. The real power in our relationship with God is in prayer.

We must remember God has given us choices and we have a choice about everything we do, including our desire to spend time with him.

God will never intervene where his children do not want him.

My Son's Cry to the Lord

I wake with a start and answer. "What" to my son's voice as he calls, "Mom."

There is no response and I think that possibly he is at the door waiting to get in the house. I get up and go to all the doors in the house and there is no one there.

I look at the clock and see that it is 2:30 am. I am sure that I have been dreaming and get back in bed. Before I lay down I grab my phone and text my son and ask him if he is alright. I do not expect an answer at this time of the night so I turn out the light and try to go back to sleep.

Morning arrives and my phone beeps. A text message has arrived from my son who says, "I am ok." I do not settle for that answer and call him immediately. When he answers I tell him he is not ok that I heard him call me last night very plainly. I then relay to him what had taken place. There is silence for a moment and then he says that he and his wife got into a bad argument about finances during the night. Words were spoken and feelings were hurt in the process and he had cried out to God for help at this time.

I ask him how much they need to get back on track and he tells me the amount he needs.

I am shocked at the amount because the miracle of this is my son does not know I keep a little stash for emergencies that might arise and the amount he relates to me is exactly the amount I have in my stash.

The voice of my son waking me in the night and the amount of the money in the stash cannot be a coincidence. God clearly had a use for that stash.

There is power in crying out to the Lord and the miracle of this message is proof that God does hear our pleas and acts quickly when we are in great need. Time and again I have seen the Lord work in my life and the lives of my children. I will never cease to be awed and thankful for his love to us.

2nd Corinthians 6:18

I will be a Father to you, and you shall be my sons and daughters, says the Lord Almighty.

An Angel to Watch over Me

I had moved hundreds of miles from family and friends and was very lonely in the city that I now called home. I was forty three years old and had never lived alone in my entire life. I was scared but determined I would survive and make it without any help.

I was living with a longtime friend until I could find work, but in the meantime I became a threat to her as I was single at the time. I never understood why she felt the way she did and was crushed by her talk with me saying that she did not want to be a part of my life anymore and to not embarrass her or myself by trying to keep the friendship alive. Rejected by a friend that had welcomed me and wanted to help me get on my feet I was crushed beyond normal hurt.

It was then I moved into an apartment of my own as I continued to seek employment. In the apartment next to mine was an elderly lady who would knock on my door and wake me up if I slept later than normal or if she did not see me out and around. She would later relate to me that she thought I might be suicidal. We became best of friends and looked to each other for help and companionship. I had more fun with Helen than I had with people my own age. I loved her dearly.

I found work and my job took me to another city close by. I still visited her spending week-ends whenever I had a chance. Then the inevitable happened and I was transferred with my job to another city hours away and my visits were few and far between. She grieved at my leaving and I missed her terribly. We sent cards and letters until there came a time there was no answer from her. Alarmed I called her daughter to ask about Helen only to be told she had passed away. My heart ached because I did not get to say good-bye to her, to tell her how much I loved her, and to thank her for being my guardian angel.

In reliving those years in my mind I truly believe that she was my guardian angel sent by God to watch over me and give me companionship during a time I was so lonely in a city where I knew no one. I thank God that I was receptive to her caring about me because I received the blessing of a friend who loved me and cared for my welfare as much as I did hers.

God does work in mysterious way his wonders to perform. I stand in awe as I think of how he loved me enough to send a friend who would heal the wounds of rejection and loneliness that was a constant part of my life and gave me a reason to get up in the morning and feel alive again.

I Miss you Helen!

Intervention from God

My heart was broken and I could not get a grip on my feelings. I had been betrayed by the person who was supposed to love me the most.

My anger roared higher and higher until I made plans to do harm to this person. I wanted revenge in the worst way to avenge the hurt that ravaged my body. My plans were made and as I drove to work the next morning my heart cried out to the Lord.

"Lord please help me for I am about to do something very stupid." As I performed my job I could feel there was something different within me. I told my co-worker that something was not right, that I felt so clean inside and the things that usually upset me were not even bothering me.

It would be two days before I would figure out what the change was. Much to my surprise my anger that had been a part of my life for a long time was gone. The anger was not only gone but the gut wrenching anger was not there.

I thought back to when this must have happened and it dawns on me that God heard my cry of distress several mornings ago and answered my prayer, not in the way I wanted it to be answered, but in the way he knew to be the best.

I wanted to get even with this person for tearing my life apart, but God wanted to show me where I needed to improve my own life. He changed me instead.

I marvel at God's handiwork within me and remember the promise he makes to us that vengeance is his. He will repay and will do far more for our cause if we have sought his help than we can ever imagine. My life has never been the same in this area since. I still get angry at times but it does not last and it has never been that gut wrenching hate anger I wrestled with for so long.

Hebrews 10: 30

For we know him who said, Vengeance is mine, I will repay." And again, "The Lord will judge his people."

Thoughts

A blue haze hangs upon the mountains hiding the valleys below.

I think of how insignificant I am gazing upon a creation near its original form, one not made or marred by man.

Mile after mile of wonders I see and I ask myself who formed them and how?

Man can only guess. My senses fill up with your closeness Lord

Songs of praise spill to my lips.

You remind me Lord that you are the mountains around me.

Here in my valley there is security and peace.

My eyes fall upon a mountain which has been tunneled through by man.

Lord, wouldn't it be nice to just tunnel through the problems we face and not have to go over the treacherous terrain?

Looking closer at the mountain the Lord shows me the scars and jagged rocks that were proof of the difficulty it took to break through to the other side.

It is then I realize no matter which road we choose to travel the road may be full of jagged rocks and full of pain.

I look ahead as the highway winds into the valley below.

A sign meets my eye which says, "Blowing sand ahead." As we drive closer sand boils into the air, wind buffets the car, and our vision is impaired.

I think about your words in the book of life, of how the foolish man built his house upon the sand. The winds blew, the storms came, and the house could not withstand.

As I remain gazing silently at the mountains your voice whispers softly in my ear about the man who built his house upon the rocks. The winds blew, the rains beat upon it, and the house stood firm.

I marvel Lord at what you have shown me and once more you fill up my senses, my heart feels your closeness, and praises spring from my lips.

The Story behind the Poem

My friend was taking a trip to Wilcox, Arizona to pick up her mother who was visiting with another daughter. She invited me to ride along with her as the drive was long and she needed someone to help her stay awake. I accepted her offer.

As we traveled that long road from Central Texas to Arizona I would write down things that impressed me along those lonely mountainous and desert roads.

Some of the sites we saw filled me with things I wanted to relate to others as I compared them to stories in the Bible.

While John Denver sang, You Fill up My Senses on the radio I began the above poem writing about the things we were seeing along the way and their relationship to God's word.

Psalms 121: 1-2

I will lift up my eyes to the mountains; from whence shall my help come?

My help comes from the Lord, who made heaven and earth.

Alone in God's Care

After months of hunting for a job I finally landed a job with a major restaurant in East Texas and was to move from a small town apartment to a city several miles away. Again I would be alone in a city where I knew no one and starting a job I had never done before in my life, managing a restaurant for David Beard's Catfish Village.

I was sad at leaving the friend I had made and our companionship, but I visited her when time permitted with my new job.

When I came to East Texas I had left behind the dearest friend a person could ever have. I had grieved for the loss of her friendship after the move and wondered when we would ever be able to once again be close enough to visit as we had before.

My friend worked at a mental health facility and was assigned a job where she traveled from city to city assessing the care and health of her clients that were housed over the state of Texas.

She would occasionally visit me, but it was with joy that she told me she had been assigned a patient that she would be assessing once a month in a facility located ten miles away. That meant she would be coming to stay with me one week-end a month. I could not contain my happiness and looked forward to each month's visit.

The months passed and I received word that I was to be transferred to another restaurant miles away from my East Texas job.

Sadness at once again losing my friend and her companionship I move to a new city to begin my job in a new restaurant.

Looking back at this time I see how unusual it was for my friend to be assigned this particular area where I was working and needing friendship and moral support, but the one thing that really got my attention was soon after my transfer the contract my friend was working in my former area was not renewed and she never went back to that facility.

Call it a coincidence, call it whatever you like, but I will always believe that God cared about me so much that he gave me a new friend and brought me my trusted friend to be a part of my life during a time when I was so lonely and out of touch with the world, just trying to keep my sanity.

I stand in awe at his love for me.

God's Care for My Child

My daughter worked the late shift at a grocery store twelve miles away in another city. She would be home around midnight sometimes a little later if she made the loop through town where all the kids hung out.

We were all in bed and I had just drifted off to sleep when suddenly I awoke with my heart pounding." Something is wrong with Louise," I say to my husband, and jump out of bed throwing my clothes on.

We drive down our country road until we get to the main highway through the area. As we turn onto the highway we see the truck she was driving beside the road.

To our horror she is not in the truck.

I am scared as we drive up and down the highway looking for her not knowing where to look or where to go.

In the process of trying to find her we meet her boyfriend's parents on the highway and learn they have had the same experience and are looking for her also. This frightens me even more.

We drive back to the truck and as we look over the vehicle we discover that she has run out of gas and did not know how to turn the switch on to the alternate tank.

While checking things over another car pulls up and we see a classmate of my children and he has my daughter with him. I am so relieved that she is ok.

Arriving back home and once again in bed I review what has just taken place. I am overcome with gratitude that God went to so much trouble to see that my child was safe and that he sent so many people to be sure of that.

God does work in mysterious ways his wonders to perform. I stand in awe of our Lord and Savior.

Psalms 9:1-2

I will give thanks to the Lord with all my heart; I will tell of all Thy wonders.

I will be glad and exalt in Thee; I will sing praise to Thy name, O most high.

Facebook Blessing

Recently I joined the Facebook fad and am amazed by all the information floating around out there among its members.

I have enjoyed touching base with those people who were a part of my life past and present and where they are in their lives has been very heartwarming.

We never know how people perceive us and I have made the statement several times that it would be nice to be able to come outside our bodies and observe ourselves as others do and be able to see what they are seeing in us.

Logging into Facebook one day I see that I have a message in my box.

Opening the message I am surprised to see it is from a cousin of mine whom I had lost touch with many years ago.

She tells me that I was her idol and of a time she visited me and I let her help me bake chocolate pies.

She proceeds to tell me I had influenced her life and was her role model.

I am blown away because never in a hundred years would I have thought I had any influence with her. This is heavy stuff for me and I wonder what I did that she used me as her role model.

I am humbled and marvel that my life could possibly influence anyone.

I thank God for this cousin who made my day and caused me to be more aware of the people I come in contact with and how I interact with them.

Emergency Double Trouble

My job was registering patients into the emergency room for treatment.

It is important to make each person feel that whatever the problem going on with them their wellbeing and health is our major focus.

One evening a young woman walks into the office and the load she is bearing is insurmountable in her eyes.

She reveals to me that her young daughter is pregnant and unmarried. As we talk she tells me she has just found out that she is going to have a baby herself. No insurance and a job not sufficient to meet these future bills. At that moment she could not see beyond the negatives of her situation.

She began coming to the emergency room for her check-ups and each time we talked I would try to have words of encouragement for her. I remarked to her that she could let this burden make her or break her, and her daughter needed her and she needed her daughter as well. This could be a bonding of moral and mental support for each other that would bring love and respect to last a life time.

After the baby came I never saw this woman again until one day seventeen years later.

Shopping in a store I hear someone call my name and look up as this woman says, "Oh, it is you, "and runs around the counter grabbing me in a big hug. She then removes her billfold and shows me photos of the babies now seventeen years old. Her pride is heartwarming to me as she remarks," if it had not been for you, I would not have made it."

Doesn't it astonish how God works? How he brings people into your life to minister to and when it is over you realize you were blessed as well.

I was to encounter this woman once more.

My husband and I attended a city council meeting to give our support for the humane society's new building program.

As we sit down someone grabs me around the neck from behind. I turn to see my friend who is saying to my husband, "I love this lady."

We visit for a few minutes and as I turn around she says," I love you."

By this time everyone is wondering what the love in is all about and staring.

God is so awesome. How could anyone know this was a time when I needed reassurance someone cared and the Lord brought this woman once more into my life to let me see that I am worthwhile and there are people who truly love me.

What an amazing God who sees our every need and supplies the answers. Maybe we do not realize it at the time, but when you reflect on the encounter it begins to register how God goes to great lengths to take care of his children.

Ecclesiastes 3: 12

I know that there is nothing better for man than to be happy and do good while they live.

Ashamed

Driving around town I was listening to my I-Pod and one of the many Gaither Homecoming series CD's that I own.

As a man begins to sing it was evident he was either retarded or had a serious speech impediment.

I was really disgusted and wondered why they would record something like this and I reached to turn the song off.

It seemed at that instant a voice tells me that I need to listen to this. I did not turn the song off but began to listen to this man sing.

Even if he could not say the words very well you could hear the joy in his voice and the love of the Lord coming from him. He was so happy to be singing for the Lord and it just poured from his every fiber.

I began weeping and thinking what an idiot I was to judge the sincerity or motives of someone's walk with God.

In my mind I could imagine the love on the Lord's face as he listened to this child sing praises to him.

The Lord had a lesson for me and I am glad I listened for I received a blessing from this man and his disability.

Matthew 7:1-2

Do not judge lest you be judged yourself. For in the way you judge, you will be judged and by your standard of measure, it shall be measured unto you.

THE JOY OF THE LORD IS MY STRENGTH

A Friend Struggles with Life

Judy struggled with life and addiction to prescription medications. As a result her children suffered and her marriage was falling apart. She felt helpless as things slowly came apart around her.

At the rough times she would always seek me out because she knew that I would not judge her and would go with her through whatever the problem she had.

At one of these times she needs to go to the emergency room and I drive her there staying with her until she is released.

As I drive her home she begs me to give her a reason to not take her life.

I panic because my knowledge of the Bible isn't the best to be answering such life and death questions.

I tell her that I feel it is against God's will for us to take our lives as you are saying that God is not big enough to handle your problems.

She wants scripture to back up why she should not take her life. I tell her I will find the scripture for her, but I need her to go to bed and get some rest and I would be back in the morning.

I went home asking God for some help in finding the comfort she needed. I spent the night sitting in my rocking chair reading the Bible for the word I was to give her.

Just as I was about to give up my eyes rested on a verse in 1st Corinthians 3:16-17.

Do you not know that you are a temple of God, and that the Spirit of God dwells in you?

If any man destroys the temple of God, God will destroy him, for the temple of God is holy, and that is what you are.

I was grateful for the word and when morning came I made my way over to her house.

She received this message from the scripture and even though she still had many problems she never tried to take her life.

In the years gone by I have wondered what happened to this friend as she never contacted me again. I only hope she found peace and happiness in her life.

Death of a Husband

I knew when Tiny and I married that he had a severe heart problem and before we met he had already had eight bypass surgeries to his credit. We were both lonely people who were surviving divorces so my sister took it upon herself to introduce us to each other by having us over for breakfast one morning.

Afterward Tiny asked me out and we dated for over a year before we were married.

Tiny was always aware of how fragile his life was and I had no comprehension of the seriousness of his condition.

We had been married over two years when Tiny came home and told me he thought he needed to go to the emergency room as he was having chest pain.

We rush around and I drive him to the hospital where his Doctor is already waiting.

After observation they put him in ICU where they decide to care flight him to Baylor hospital in Dallas, Texas. He is to undergo surgery to determine the damage of this heart attack.

The horror of those hours and his insensitive children is still hard for me to think about and for years I would not dare go there in my thoughts because it was so painful.

As I visited him each day he became agitated. There was something he was trying to say to me and the breathing tube down his throat kept him from conveying his need to me.

He wrote unreadable notes and made signs, but it was when he raised his hands in a prayerful hold under his chin I realized what he wanted.

Tiny growing up and even into adulthood had never been to Church at all until he married me. So it is with awe and fear I pursued this request praying for God to give me the right words to say.

I ask him if he wants the Chaplain and he shakes his head no. I then ask him if he wants us to pray for him and he shakes his head yes. I realize there are dialogues going on between him and the Lord because he writes a note I can read and it says, "The Lord says that he does not have a place for me right now."

What do you say to a remark like this?

I begin talking to him telling him that he does not have to get out of bed and kneel down, that he can talk to God right where he is and tell him what he needs to tell him and if he has anything he feels was wrong in his life to ask forgiveness and request to be remembered in God's house.

I tell him that my son's church is praying for him as well as friends in the community.

That prayer is going up for him. This seems to bring him peace and he shakes his head yes.

It would be days later that they take the tube from him and he relates to me that God told him that now he has a place for him and proceeds to tell me I was a good wife and he is worried about me if something happens to him.

The Doctor tells the family there is no hope for him to go home and Tiny and him have an agreement between them that the Doctor will keep him pain free as he dies. One thing the Doctor says is that he is worried about me and cannot let go because of this.

The Doctor then tells me I have to go and reassure him it is ok for him to die. These words stun me and I think how I can give permission for him to die when I want him to live.

We all gather in the ICU room where he is and bravely with no tears I tell him that it is alright for him to go, that I will be ok, and he must not worry about me. He asks me to rub his legs as they are cold and as I do he sighs and is gone.

The funeral and the aftermath of his death is a blur. I cannot remember making arrangements or very few conversations or happenings over the next few months. I was in limbo for a long time.

One night I was awakened and as I lay there a poem began running through my mind and I knew I had to get up and write this down it was so strong.

Tiny was a trucker most of his life and this is the Poem that the Lord gave me in the wee morning hours to honor him.

The Last long Haul

He pulled into the weigh station along the journey he sped to complete.

His destination was in sight.

How he longed to walk those golden streets.

He climbs from the cab with the name Tiny engraved in gold.

He shades his eyes for the light is so bright.

Then he sighs for his fuel is running mighty low.

Climbing back into the cab he roars the engine, impatient at the delay.

Then he lets up on the clutch spinning and throwing gravel along the way.

Puffs of smoke pour from the stacks.

The engine strains beneath the load this trip.

Perspiration runs from his brow, while dreams of cool water from the well of life he soon will sip.

"Breaker one nine, Calling St. Peter," he breaks in to say.

"This is Tiny. I'm coming home." "I'm gonna drop this load today."

His smile grows wide as St. Peter replies.

Pedal to the metal son you have my okay.

The golden arches swing wide as he draws near and convoys of eighteen wheelers suddenly appear.

In the lead blaring down on the horn are Mom and Dad welcoming their son who is weary and worn.

He jumps down from the cab and hands St. Peter the keys.

"Won't need these," he says, "I just finished my last run."

He looks back and gives a wave to those he left behind.

His course is finished his race is won.

Tiny's Prayer

He prayed, "Father come and heal my broken spirit. I need to feel the touch of your hands," and he prayed," Savior I am coming home to you. My course is finished, my race is won."

Message from a Spanking

I was babysitting my young granddaughter when she had a little fit because something did not go her way.

I swatted her bottom where upon she began to cry. I knew I had not hurt her and after ignoring her tears for a while and hearing the crying getting louder and louder I say to her, "Michelle what is wrong with you?" "Why are you crying so hard?"

Her tear stained face looks up at me and says, "You don't love me anymore."

"Wait," That is not true Michelle," I say.

"I love you very much and that will never change, I just did not like or love what you just did when you had your fit, "but I will always love you."

She stops crying and looks at me with wonder in her eyes as she replies, "Oh Grandma, I get it." "I was afraid you did not love me."

From that moment on she never feared being disciplined. Yes she cried, but it never lasted long and she was on her way to other things.

I think about Our Heavenly Father and his love for us. He disciplines us because he loves us and wants us to be Godly.

Hebrews 12:5-7

And you have forgotten the exhortation which is addressed to you as sons.

"My son do not regard lightly the discipline of the Lord, nor faint when you are reproved by him;

For those whom the Lord loves he disciplines, and He scourges every son whom He receives."

It is for discipline that you endure; God deals with you as with sons; for what son is there whom his father does not discipline?

I-Pods and Mustard Seeds

My husband bought me a new I-Pod for Christmas. The newest at the time just off the market was called the Nano.

I opened this small package and looking inside I had no idea what this small blue three inch square was.

When I asked," What is this?" my granddaughter replied," It's an I-Pod grandma."

I began to read the instructions on this item and it was amazing to me that something this small could hold over a thousand songs within it. When I thought of how many records or cassettes that would add up to I was impressed all over again.

Thinking about the I-Pod I was reminded of Jesus's words in Matthew 13:31-32 when he talks about the mustard seed.

He presented another parable to them saying, "The kingdom of heaven is like the mustard seed which a man took and planted in his field."

"And this is smaller than all other seeds; but when it is full grown, it is larger than the garden plants, and becomes a tree, so that the birds of the air come and nest in its branches."

Holding that small square in my hands my thoughts were, if the mustard seed and this I-Pod can produce such dramatic results just think what a small amount of faith can produce when we are grounded in the Lord.

Leave Me Alone, But don't Go Away

My friend Sandy was having a difficult time.

It seemed she was bombarded from every side with every problem imaginable and now the time had come that she was going to have to make serious decisions that would affect her life and those around her for many years to come.

She asked my advice and I wanted to tell her how I felt and how she should handle the problems at hand in order to accomplish the best results.

My tongue was silent and I found my love and support was all I had to offer her in return for the question she asked of me.

After all that was really what she wanted.

In anger because I would not give her the answer she sought she lashes out at me and says," Leave me alone," then as an afterthought she says," but don't go away."

As I thought about what she had said to me I was reminded of our relationship with God.

We basically keep him at arm's length, but our hearts are begging him to stay.

We want to be sure we have arms to run to, a shoulder to cry on, and a home to come home to in time of need.

And he promised us those things.

I asked myself why we are always forgetting where our strength comes from?

Matthew 11:29-30

"Take my yoke upon you, and learn from me, for I am gentle and humble in heart; and you shall find rest for your souls."

"For my yoke is easy, and my load is light."

www.ingramcontent.com/pod-product-compliance
Lightning Source LLC
Chambersburg PA
CBHW031331040426
42443CB00005B/297